International Library of Philosophy and Theology

(MODERN THINKERS SERIES: David H. Freeman, *Editor*)

NIETZSCHE

by

VAN RIESSEN

Translated by Dirk Jellema

PRESBYTERIAN AND REFORMED PUBLISHING CO.
PHILLIPSBURG, NEW JERSEY
1978

CONTENTS

BRIEF BIBLIOGRAPHY

Menschliches, Allzumenschliches, ein Buch für freie Geister, 1878

Also sprach Zarathustra, 1883

Jenseits von Gut und Böse, 1886

Zur Genealogie der Moral, 1887

Die Götzendämmerung, 1888

Der Wille zur Macht, Versuch einer Umwertung aller Werte, 1888

Ecce homo, 1888

* * * * *

For a fuller bibliography see:
Karl Jaspers—*Nietzsche* p. 411ff. (Berlin, 1936).

THE AUTHOR

Dr. H. Van Riessen is the author of this Modern Thinkers Series monograph on Nietzsche. A prominent member of a school of philosophy that has developed in the Netherlands under the leadership of Herman Dooyeweerd, Van Riessen himself might well be the subject matter of a future essay in this series. Holding graduate degrees in both engineering and philosophy, he is a professor at the Institute of Technology of Delft in the Netherlands.

An active participant in the Underground Movement during the German occupation, Van Riessen understands the agonies of social and cultural change from personal experience. An engineer, scientist, philosopher and statesman, he is active in political, social, and economic movements in the Netherlands.

Dr. Van Riessen is the author of many articles as well as a major scientific and philosophic work, *Philosophy and Technique*. In this country where he has lectured extensively, he is best known for his *The Society of the Future* (translated by David H. Freeman and published by the Presbyterian and Reformed Publishing Co.).

This monograph originally appeared as a chapter in *Modern Thinkers*, a publication of Wever (Franeker), edited by Dr. Zuidema. It was translated for the International Library of Theology and Philosophy by Dr. Dirk Jellema of the Case Institute of Technology.

NIETZSCHE

Have you understood me? Dionysius against
the Crucified One....
Ecce Homo
Dionysius against the Crucified One: there
you have the Antithesis.
The Will to Power.

I. THE THEME

The work of this great thinker, who chose such a radical and courageous position in the struggle of ideologies, as the twentieth century dawned, cannot be adequately covered in these few pages. Hence the reader should expect to encounter only Nietzsche's basic ideas. And even at that, the reader will meet only the shadow of Nietzsche, for it is impossible for me to reproduce in my words that intensity with which Nietzsche poured out his passions.

For that, you must read Nietzsche himself. Then you can begin to understand how his bruised and rebellious heart suffered and fought. For he holds none of this back from the reader. And he can give such a sublime and compelling account of this that it is difficult to find a philosopher who can match his style.

What is it that agitates Nietzsche so deeply? He is a child of his time, and his time was the calm before the storm. He stands, in that calm, as the *prophet* of the coming century, our century. But most important is this in Nietzsche, that he sees the *choice* which modern man would face in that coming century; and that he himself makes his choice, courageously, radically and logically — even though his choice meant that he himself, in a sense, must perish.

Nietzsche chooses for Dionysius and against Christ, the Crucified One. He chooses this earth as over against the Kingdom of Heaven. He chooses for *life*, for that intoxicating, unchained, overflowing, creating, boundless, savage, brute *life*, which makes its own laws. That life is symbolized for him by the Greek god Dionysius. And in some places Nietzsche realizes that this is also the Antichrist.

9

That, then, is the central, the religious theme of his life. We shall see later how he came to hold this position, and to what conclusions and problems this position brought him. Anyone who has grasped the basic meaning of humanism — the denial of the crucified Christ as Savior of the world — will understand why I call Nietzsche the *radical humanist*. He strips humanism of all its frills, of everything in it which tends towards a synthesis with Christianity: for he realizes that any position which tries to compromise between following Christ and following Dionysius is untenable, and doomed to disappear: and he realizes, too, that the time for the end of compromise has now dawned.

There are some who would deny Nietzsche the right to call himself a philosopher. His paradoxes, exaggerations, and inner contradictions, the unsystematic character of his views — these are, these critics say, in conflict with the scholarly character of philosophy, in conflict with the clear, balanced, systematized, logical, methodical activity of reason: and hence Nietzsche cannot be called a philosopher. Undoubtedly, there is some truth in such criticisms. Though Nietzsche's works exhibit a more ordered structure than is usually realized, he is still an irrationalist. He disqualifies both reason and systematic knowledge. For him, true philosophy is *action*. And hence such criticisms would not have impressed him much; for he sought something else than a scholarly system, something more than mere reason

Perhaps he also understood that humanism in philosophy always means something different, something more, something more essential, than merely a philosophy which regards itself (thanks to the self-sufficiency of reason, or of scientific method) as unassailable. It also means and implies the self-sufficiency and unassailability and sovereignty and value of *man*, who grounds himself in and strengthens himself by such a philosophy of reason. Yes, Nietzsche undoubtedly did realize this: and when it became clear to him that reason was *not* unassailable and self-sufficient, and that science is not sovereign in its objectivity but depends on human goals, then Nietzsche threw overboard this ballast of humanism, and he pushed ahead to what he took to be the essence of humanism: the living man, who is *himself* self-sufficient, who makes the law *himself*, who *himself* is sovereign.

Nietzsche proclaimed the man, who maintains *himself* as sovereign over against Christ who preached a *lost* humanity, a humanity whose salvation is possible only through His crucifixion and resurrection.

Rationalism camouflages the choice facing modern man; positivism ignores it, Nietzsche faces it squarely. He comes to an open confrontation of the arch-enemy of the idea of an independent and sovereign humanity which can save itself. He puts himself in a position of radical opposition to Jesus, though he sometimes seems to respect him. Until the end of his life he fought him implacably, though this Jesus was in the deepest sense a riddle to Nietzsche.

II. THE MAN

Nietzsche was born in 1844 at Röcken, in Germany. His father, who died in 1849, not long after Nietzsche's birth, was a minister, and both parents came from ministers' families. Nietzsche, who had a low opinion of the Germans (even though he exepted much from them in the future), was proud of his Polish origin on his father's side.

As a boy, Nietzsche was regarded as a pious youngster, character- ized by his honesty and self-control. His high measure of intelligence and his talent for music were early noticeable. These brought about his placement in a private secondary school, where he was given a rigorous and disciplined training. He was already developing into an independent thinker at this time. Emerson was the philosopher who attracted him the most, and he was also partial to the music of Wagner.

Nietzsche intended to become a minister, and he began the study of theology at Bonn in 1864. But he was already so hesitant about accepting Christianty, and so allured by Greek culture, that he soon decided to choose classical philology as his main field of study. He did not like Bonn very well, and after a year he moved on to Leipzig.

A letter to his sister, written a few months before the move, shows how Nietzsche's critical study of Christianity was bringing him to a spiritual crisis, in which he felt himself placed before a choice between the peace of soul to be found in Christianity and the truth to be found in science and scholarship. If it was scholarly knowledge which brought him to this crisis — and he later fiercely turned against its pretensions — then it was the philosophy of Schopenhauer (whose main work he obtained by chance while at Leipzig) which helped him over the crisis, and turned his thoughts in a new direction.

Schopenhauer: self-contempt, self-castigation, the worship of art and genius — that was what appealed to Nietzsche at this point. Later he turned away from Schopenhauer also, for Schopenhauer viewed the negation of volition as the highest goal, and for the later Nietzsche, the philosopher of the will to power, that was almost as bad as the gospel of Christ.

In 1868, at Leipzig, Nietzsche met and became acquainted with the noted German composer, Wagner. The influence that this man exercised on Nietzsche was great. The young philosopher saw in Wagner his ideal: a man of true mold, and an artist who awakened the noblest in his audiences.

The following year Nietzsche was appointed (even before he obtained his doctoral degree) as professor of philology at Basel, in Switzerland. There for years he continued his friendship with Wagner, and also became a friend of the historian of culture, Burkhardt — one of the few men who retained Nietzsche's respect in later years.

Nietzsche took part in the Franco-Prussian War of 1870 as a volunteer stretcher-bearer, and as a result contracted a serious illness.

His first great publication, *The Birth of Tragedy*, appeared in 1872. This was followed by other writings, for example a series in support of Wagner's dream of a great opera center at Bayreuth. But in 1876, after Nietzsche attended a presentation of a Wagnerian opera at Bayreuth, he broke with Wagner, and there after began a fanatical attack on him. He saw clearly the element of falseness in Wagner's endeavors, and the attempt to win popular favor; and he was hurt above all by *Parsifal* which he saw as an attempt at compromising with Christianity. He felt that this was a betrayal of their common ideals. "Wagner has become pious," he wrote in disgust.

Nietzsche during this period was seriously ill. He was tormented by terrible headaches, and his mental health was also weakened. This was a forewarning of his later insanity. Nevertheless, he turned out three important books during these years.

In 1879 Nietzsche, who must have been an inspiring teacher, gave up his professorial position. This was partially because of ill health, but also because he felt that academic life was interfering with his true life work. After 1879 he withdrew from society and worked in secluded surroundings, living either in the Alps or in Northern Italy. After 1882 there was a slow improvement in his health, but the solitude in which he lived and worked became steadily greater — and despite his craving for human companionship, he helped ensure this solitude by his outspoken works and his bitter attacks on earlier friends.

Between 1882 and 1888 Nietzsche wrote his most important books, among them *Thus Spake Zarathustra, Beyond Good and Evil, The Genealogy of Morals, The Antichrist,* and *Ecce Homo.* These last two were published later; and the same is true of the work he had planned as his philosophical *magnum opus, The will to Power.* Nietzsche never completed it, and it was pieced together later from the plans and fragments he left.

Then, in 1889, his incipient insanity suddenly broke through. Some of his friend received letters signed "The Crucified One." One such letter, written to his friend Brandes, in a childish hand and on pencil-lined paper, reads: "To friend George. After you had discovered me, it was no great masterpiece to find me. The great difficulty now is to lose me. The Crucified One."

The sick and insane Nietzsche was faithfully cared for by his mother, and later, until his death in 1900, by his sister.

Who was this brilliant man, really? What was the cause of his insanity? What relation was there between his insanity and his work? Even apart from the problem of whether a complete answer can be given to such questions, such an answer would neither be within my capabilities nor part of my task in these few pages. But, I do want to make a few remarks, for these questions do force themselves upon us.

We can trace, with little difficulty, the presence of a highly nervous and over-excited spirit in Nietzsche's life and works; a spirit which inclined to extremes and which did not know how to reconcile them. The man who sought and preached solitude was also the man who longed passionately for human friendship. The man who could be such an affable social companion was also the man who saw in war a remedy for our sick culture: "The man must be brought up for war, the woman for the relaxation of the man. All else is foolishness." The man who was noted for his generosity also taught that the weak should be annihilated. In social gatherings he was modesty and amia-bility personified but as soon as he took up the pen he attacked his fellow men — in general, and also personally — in the most galling ways imaginable. And while he let pass no chance to give vent to his contempt of women, it was two women who alone loved and respected him during his period of solitude: his mother and his sister.

And not only that. Anyone who reads *Ecce Homo* can hardly avoid feeling that Nietzsche has lost all sense of proportion. The book is from 1888, and Nietzsche begins it with these remarks: "In view of the fact that I am about to present humanity with the most weighty chal-lenge ever placed before it, it appears to me unavoidable that I must explain who I am." And than follow such chapter titles as "Why I am So Wise," "Why I am So Clever," "Why I Write Such Good Books" and "Why I am a Destiny."

Such headings do not leave much doubt about the contents of the book, which are often similar in tone. In the last chapter, for example, he says "I am by far the most dreadful man who has ever existed; but that does not exclude that I shall be the most beneficial."

Still at all, to see in this merely the results of mental disturbance is to make a grave mistake. Rather, sickness has peeled off the protective covering of this man, who neither conceived nor wished any possible course of action than to glorify man: to glorify himself. That was his religion. It was in that way that he understood his ideal, the *Uebermensch*, the Superman; and it was in that way that he portrayed Zarathustra, with whom he more and more identified himself. In the terrible struggle to attach some real significance and meaning to the idea that man is self-sufficient, that man is his own standard, that man can love only his own destiny in the struggle to find some anchorage in this position, Nietzsche's mind crumbled.

Hence also to say that an organic disease — inherited, due to infection, or whatever — destroyed Nietzsche's powers and limited his writings, is to oversimplify. No, his works are primarily the residue, the deposit, from a terrible spiritual struggle. And the hopelessness of this struggle certainly helped bring about his insanity.

III. THE DEVELOPMENT OF NIETZSCHE'S IDEAS

It goes without saying that Nietzsche's view underwent a process of development, and this is true also of the period when he was publishing his works, a period of some nineteen years. There have been various attempts to divide this development into periods. The division which appeals most to me is a division into three periods, the first ending in 1876 at the break with Wagner, and the third beginning in 1882 with the publication of *Thus Spake Zarathustra*.

But this division does not mean much more to me than the simple recognition of youthful period (with its aesthetic ideals), a transitional period (in which he distinguished his real views from these ideals, and purified his thought by removing what he judged were decadent ideals), and a final period-in which he expressed his outlook clearly and sharply (in his struggle to retain not only the nihilism which he regarded as inescapable, but also an affirmative attitude towards life; and in his fight against Jesus, his encounter with Him whom he regarded as his greatest enemy).

The relation between these three periods is to be understood as a process of increasing concentration on the essential problems, and an increasingly radical presentation of alternatives. This radicalizing of presentation can be noted in Nietzsche's changing style of writing. He wrote nearly everything as aphorisms, short and more or less independent pieces. But these aphorisms become less and less reasoned; they become increasingly shorter; and in his later period even the sentences hold more and more ideas in an increasingly compressed form.

This increased compression of thought is largely caused by the fact that Nietzsche's sight was becoming worse and worse, so that as he walked, almost blind, and meditated, he concentrated his thoughts to the utmost. He remarked, correctly, that he knew how to express in ten sentences what another man could not express in a book. On the other hand, not only the increasingly concentrated form but also the increasingly alarming content of his writings should be noted. The sentences in which he pours out his hate and his passions and his love as longings become biting, flashing, explosive.

I would therefore not agree with those who stress the division of Nietzsche's development into sharply defined periods according to different philosophical characteristics. Naturally, we can distinguish various periods, but that means merely that the emphasis of Nietzsche's thought rests first on one thing and then on another. With the passage of time this simply becomes more accentuated.

As regards his views of science (Wissenschaft), during his student days Niezsche expected much help from it in his search for truth; but after that period, its importance for him grew less and less. In any event, we can view him to begin with as an irrationalist, who viewed science (Wissenschaft) pragmatically, as a servant of life, who depreciated the value of reason. He took as his philosophic exemplar the enigmatic Heraclitus, the philosopher of becoming, who saw in the strife of opposites the basic principle of life, the philosopher who tried to fathom destiny. Parmenides, imprisoned in the snares of his own logic, is his opposite, a philosopher as icy as Heraclitus is fiery. And Socrates, with his moralizing reason, which Plato (says Nietzsche) picked up from the gutter, is for Nietzsche a figure of horror, the horror of the decadence of Greece, so like the decadence of the West.

He soon became convinced also that the power of the intellect lies in a sort of camouflaging process, and that the orderly laws of science have content only insofar as we ourselves impose this order on nature, and that the systems of Wissenschaft serve merely as a protection for life.

Philosophy, for Nietzsche, is not an abstract thing, not a systematic structure. For him, its character is that of a deed, of an art; and its goal is Life.

Dionysius plays a leading role as early as The Birth of Tragedy. He personifies the dynamic "Yes!" to life, the eternal drive towards the becoming of life; that drive which rises beyond horror and suffering, which carries within itself the will to annihilation.

Nietzsche contrasts with this the Apollinian motif. He sees this as a kind of aesthetic therapy which tries to hold the lawlessness and ecstacy of life within the bonds of harmony, which tries to maintain eternal beauty over against self-annihilating life. It is only as regards this point that we can speak of a clear break in the development of Nietzsche's thought. For it was after the quarrel with Wagner, after the collapse of his idealized picture of Wagner, the personification of this Apollonian ideal of a pure and elevating art, that he turned his back on art and artistic emotion.

Nietzsche, in his solitude, turned to intensive self-examination, and he prepared himself (in this period of severe bodily suffering) for the new road he must follow by first getting rid of all remnants of romanticism and sentimentality.

The emphasis then shifted to a positivistic approach. Only the real, the facts, possess any value. The *Umwertung aller Werte*, the transvaluation of all values, begins. God is dead. Christ is the enemy of life, morality is a lie, truth is a fiction. And that which remains is the Dionysius life, life without illusions and sham, a destiny which men must joyously accept.

Then there arises out of this life a new type of man. "Friend Zarathustra came, the guest of all guests." And Nietzsche also turns to nihilism, for nihilism is the lack of all values. and an affirmation of the meaninglessness of all existence. No matter what theme he afterwards took up — the masters and the herd, the will to power as the basic motif of life, the Superman — Nietzsche neither wished nor was able to break away from this nihilism. The highest form of the dynamic "Yes!" to Life, for the later Nietzsche, was the eternal recurrence, the eternal return to nothingness.

So, apart from the one noticeable break with his earlier ideas which we have mentioned above, it is not the different periods but rather the continuity of Nietzsche's thought which we should emphasize. Even at the beginning we encounter all his basic themes, and where he contradicts himself — for example, in his treatment of free will — such contradictory statements group themselves around the basic themes as illustrations of the inner contradictions of irrationalism, and indeed as illustrations of the hopelessness of Nietzsche's attempt to find a firm anchorage in nihilism.

In *Thus Spake Zarathustra*, Nietzsche compares the different periods in the growth of the spirit to three things; the camel, the lion, and the child. That is, the camel, who lets himself be loaded down, with the burden of *Wissenschaft* (scientific and scholarly knowledge); the lion, who bravely frees himself from this compulsion and others

16

like it; and finally the child, who does not let himself be burdened with history and guilt, but who gives a joyous and unashamed assent to life. And although Nietzsche himself never fully experienced the last of these periods, the childlike acceptance of life, his analogy can be viewed as a useful description of his own spiritual development.

Nietzsche in his *Ecce Homo* explained the meaning and the aim of a number of his earlier books, and it may be useful for an understanding of his spiritual development and of his aims to quote from a few of these evaluations.

Regarding his *Birth of Tragedy*, Nietzsche says (among other things): "This, my first effort, was remarkable beyond measure. I had revealed the only and its counterpart (i.e., Dionysius and Apollo) which history offers — and thus I was the first to comprehend the wonderful phenomenon of the Dionysian Life." And further: "Those elements of existence which the Christian and other nihilists reject, take infinitely higher rank in the hierarchy of values then those approved of by the instinct of decadence, these it only may call good." "An awesome hope is voiced in this work." "Let us look ahead a century; let us assume that my onslaughts on two thousand years of opposition to nature, and of degradation of humanity, have been successful. Every new partner of life, having as his task the greatest of all tasks, the cultivation and development of a higher humanity, as well as the relentless destructions of everything degenerate and parasitical, every partner will re-establish a superabundance of life, from which the Dionysian state must rise once again. I predict an age of tragedy."

Thoughts Out of Season (1873–1876), says Nietzsche, was a series of essays. The first of them (1873) is an attack on German culture, which had become a culture without meaning, without content, without aim; it was merely a kind of public opinion. The second essay (1874) was written to expose the poisonous and sapping influence of modern *Wissenschaft*. The aim, culture, is lost sight of; and the means *Wissenschaft*, becomes barbarized. In the third and fourth essays (1874, 1876), Nietzsche gives two pictures of men whose lives might serve as pointers to a higher culture; men who were vigorously self-disciplined and egotistical, men full of contempt for "Empire," "Success," "Christianity," "Culture," and the other catchwords of the day: they were Schopenhauer and Wagner (who at that time were still in Nietzsche's favor).

Nietzsche sees his *Human, All Too Human* (1878, 1880) as a record of crisis in his development, a crisis which had to prduce its own cure: the purging away of ideals and sentiment, for these are human, all too human. Only when this purgation is completed can the truly free spirit make its appearance. This was written during Nietzsche's liberation from the thought of Schopenhauer and Wagner, from what he called those higher forms of fraud, from idealism, sentimentality, and other femininities.

With *The Dawn of Day* (1881), says Nietzsche he began his campaign against morality — for morality is prejudices, "automatized" prejudiced. "This yea-saying book. . . . sends out its light and love and tenderness over all evil things, and gives them back their spirit, their serenity of conscience, their high right and privilege of existence.

Then came *The Joyous Wisdom* (1882), which he judges as a yea-saying book of the highest degree, in which profundity and high spirits are delicately combined. Here is the first formulation of a destiny for all ages.

In *Thus Spake Zarathustra* (1883–1888), in which the Eternal Recurrence, the cycle of cosmic existences, is the basic theme, Nietzsche pictures the yea-saying man, the man of the future. That means for him the truly healthy man, the Dionysian man. "At every moment in these lines, the idea of man is surpassed, and the concept of the Superman takes on the greatest reality." This is the most profound book which humanity possesses, says Nietzsche.

Beyond Good and Evil (1886) is an attack on modernity, directed against modern *Wissenschaft* (science and scholarship), modern art, modern politics, and so forth; an attack on everything modern man is proud of — his "sense of history," his tolerance, his objectivity, his pity for the weak and suffering.

Three things are taken up in *The Genealogy of Morals*. First, the birth of Christianity from the resentment of the weak against the strong; then, the psychology of sentiment and conscience; and, finally, the reason for the power of the priest-ideal, which for Nietzsche is the will to annihilation of life, and the essence of decadence. This Power is not due to God, for He does not exist; rather, says Nietzsche it is explained by the fact that there has been no real alternative; the opposite ideal, Zarathustra, was lacking.

The Twilight of the Idols is praised by Nietzsche as a wonderful statement of the vanishing of the old "truths," which were really idols. "There is no book more rich in substance, more independent, more subversive — more wicked."

So far, then, Nietzsche's evaluation of his books, as given in *Ecce Homo*. These were followed by *The Antichrist*, which he planned to use as the first chapter of his proposed main work, *The Will to Power*.

That work, which he was unable to finish, was later pieced together from his many notations and plans regarding it.

If you can ignore Nietzsche's absurdities and contradictions, you will encounter in his books a man who poured out his whole heart in his philosophy; a man who suffered as he examined himself and the times in which he lived, a man who was led by his insight and his honesty to seek a way out for himself and for his age; a man who became more and more entangled and enmeshed, and who fought more and more bitterly to free himself.

It was opposed to Nietzsche's very nature to seek a cheap peace in a compromise, or to grasp that temptation which philosophy can offer — the temptation to avoid coming to grips with the problem by seeking refuge in an intellectual abstraction.

Nietzsche realized, as is clear when he is examined closely, that the ninetheenth century, the century of progress, was decadent, indeed, that the modern idea of progress was itself a decadent idea. And he saw too what would emerge from this decadence: nihilism. "Nihilism stands before the door. From whence came this most gruesome of guests?" He wants us to understand also the origin of this nihilism.

Indeed, besides being the prophet of nihilism, Nietzsche wishes also to be a priest of nihilism. He judges himself as decadent, and incapable of doing more than offering himself to the coming nihilism, that he judged to be the only way to the future. Only by becoming the prophet and priest of nihilism could Nietzsche help the coming of the Kingdom of This World, which he opposed to the Kingdom he felt to be a lie, the Kingdom of Heaven, of which Christ prophesied and for which he suffered in his priestly capacity.

Let us now see what it was that so aroused Nietzsche's ire, and how he understood that which he attacked.

IV. THE PROPHET OF NIHILISM

All thóse marks of what people in our day call progress — success, peace, toleration, equality, helpfulness, neighborliness, democracy, socialism, technology — are viewed by Nietzsche as the very things which are the marks of *decadence*, signs of vanished vitality. He understood how false and rotten and lukewarm the life of his day was. Because of Christian ideals, he thought; because men have cut themselves off from Christ, and have deified man, we say. There we part company with Nietzsche.

The ideal of progress, says Nietzsche, is that eventually there will be nothing more to fear. Technology will bring this about. But, in fact, it is fear which has made man great and produced his culture. The whole sphere of business and industry is low and shallow: prosperity has made man powerless: it is not wild animals we must fear, but the man of the hospital: and so forth. Modern man can no longer distinguish between those things which help him and those which damage him. Consider only the division of his time, the choice of his associations, his work, his relaxation, his commands and his obedience, his eating and sleeping, his thinking. "We modern men, so tender and sentimental, giving and receiving a hundred courtesies, we tell ourselves that this amiable humanity which we represent, this unanimous agreement on leniency, willingness to help, mutual dependence — that this is a mark of progress, and that by all this we have risen far above the men of the Renaissance!"

That equality which Rousseau preached is honored: and men make noble pleas for that neighborly love which can bring it about. But what has vanished, cries Nietzsche, is the love of man for *himself.* "We castigate this tainted freedom, the weak compromise, the whole virtuous filthiness of the modern 'yes and no,' the tolerance which forgives everything because it understands everything."

Nietzsche sees all this as showing and resulting from the *weakness of will* in modern man, ruled as he is by doubts and restlessness. Man no longer knows the independence of decision, the brave joy of willing. Most of those things which are, so to speak, on proud exhibit in the display windows of our civilization — objectivity, certain and unbased knowledge, scholarship, *l'art pour l'art* — these things are really exhibitions of polished skepticism and paralysis of the will. This is shown also in the scholarly study of history. Men dig deep into the past simply because they have no perspective of the future. But it is exactly our excessive knowledge of the past which paralyzes us. We must therefore pose this question: how much knowledge of history is necessary for life?

Nietzsche realized clearly that there are no objective facts, no brute facts, but only interpreted facts. In this and other similar protests against the *Zeitgeist,* the spirit of the age, his often masterfully hard-hitting style is coupled with a reference to his own position, from which he views the facts and explains their origin.

As concerns the origin of the facts of our contemporary situation, he thinks that we have put ourselves in an impasse through our belief in a kind of general truth, *in a morality,* and along with that, in free will. Man proposes the idea of a free will so that he can differentiate between good deeds and good men, and bad deeds and bad men. He tests goodness and badness by his system of morality. But to Nietzsche morality is merely a necessary lie. The animal in man likes to be beguiled.

Where does morality come from? Nietzsche answers that morality, and the establishment of a system of truth which prevails throughout a given society, arises from the herd-man's need of protection against the masters. This morality of utility, says Nietzsche, has no connection with the so-called love of one's neighbor; its motives are not love, but fear and hope. Morality is nothing more than the protective instinct of the *herd* in its struggle against the masters: the struggle of the suffering against the successful; of the mediocre against the exceptional. "Morality in Europe today is herd-morality."

Master-morality is something completely different. And it is the special right of the masters to create values which serve them. According to slave-morality, a master who arouses fear in his servants is bad; but according to master-morality, the master who arouses fear is good, and the lovable master is contemptible.

Thus what form morality takes depends solely on the demands of this *strife* between the masters and the herd, between the strong and the weak. There is no general measuring-stick, nor is there a free will which can do "good" or "bad" things according to such a measuring-stick. There is nothing more than strong wills and weak wills; what men call morality is simply an adjustment to one or the other of these.

But Darwin was wrong, says Nietzsche (and Darwin influenced him in this whole outlook on morality), when he assumed that the strongest will always win out. For at present, the sheep have mastered the hawk. And this being the case, the herd-virtues of amiability, industry, moderation and pity have become the prevailing measuring-stick.

That the herd was inspired to conquer the masters, is to be blamed on the *priests*, the religious leaders. These men tamed the animal in man. What drove them to action was their hatred of the masters, a hatred caused by their feeling of inferiority and weakness. Therefore they joined with the herd, by developing a common religion, so that they could lead the slave revolt.

Their method was highly subtle. They said that suffering was noble — and thus put the suffering herd-man on a pedestal. They proclaimed salvation and eternal life — and thus inspired the herd with hope. Whatever helped increase their power, they called the will of God; and whatever they viewed as important, they named the Kingdom of God.

In recent centuries the priests have had to make room for the *philos-*

ophers. Kant and the rest. But the philosophers simply continued the tradition and the corruption of the priests. They too adopted the rule as a protection against the exception. They made morality self-sufficient, in the name of reason, and they gave up the so-called truth of the old religious myths. The result was a pale counterfeit of religion; but a counterfeit minted, nevertheless, from a die fashioned by the priests.

In the background of all this discussion, Nietzsche regards *Christianity* as the greatest disaster for true culture. We shall see later whether or not Nietzsche gives a one-sided picture of Christianity, but in any event Christianity for him includes all types of decadence. Humanity must now pay for two thousand years of Christianity.

Christianity, inspired by the hatred of the weak against the strong, has carried on a war to the death against the higher type of man; it would conquer the mighty beast of prey by poisoning him. In this it has been successful. But in order to preserve everything that was sick and suffering, to bring about the "deterioration" of the European race, it was necessary for Christianity to stand all true values on their head. It taught scepticism of all true values. The god of decadence is the god of the weak; and weak call themselves the good. But they are simply those who have no feeling for power. The amount of belief a man finds necessary is a measure of his weakness. "My word '*immorality*' fundamentally refers to two denials. I deny, first, a type of man who until now has been valued highly, the *good* man, the *kind* man, the *charitable* man; and, second, the kind of morality which in itself has come to be the prevailing and dominant morality — the morality of decadence; or, more clearly, the *Christian* morality."

Christianity consists of sheer fictions. God, the soul, free will, sin, punishment, grace, repentance, temptation, the Kingdom of God, eternal life — all are purely imaginary. What actually determines the course of our life? — a drop of blood more or less in the brains: but Christianity seeks the controlling cause in sin and the devil.

Nietzsche gives a very striking expression of his bitter hatred for Christianity when he describes (in *The Genealogy of Morals*) the subterranean workshop where the ideals of Christianity are manufactured. In this imaginary workshop, weakness are made into merits; feebleness distorted into goodness; fear-filled groveling into humility; submission to those whom you hate, into obedience, because God wills it. To be incapable of getting revenge is called not wishing to get revenge. Those who toil in this workshop exist in wretchedness; but they call this "election," for does not a man chastise the dog he loves best, and besides, this wretched existence is a testing and preparation for the eternal blessedness which will more than make up for it. They whisper among themselves that they are not only better than the masters of the earth — whose boots they must lick (not out of fear, of course, but because God commands them to be obedient to the authorities!) — but that they possess more, and in any event will obtain more. The masterpiece of this black art, concludes Nietzsche, the most subtle refinement of these hate-filled cellar-animals, is that they say that they are righteous, and that they hate injustice, and that they and their brothers hope for justice instead of rewards, and are filled with love rather than hate! Their solace for all their suffering is the Last Judgment, and until then, they say, they live in faith, hope, and love!

The most dangerous of the fabrications of Christianity is *pity*. Nietzsche sees in this greatest of vices simply a weakness of will, which results in the will's losing itself in harmful sentimentality.

The reader should not be too quick to become annoyed with, or amused at, this jeering and hate-filled Nietzsche, nor too quick to turn away from him and his attack on Christianity. For it is all true, everything that Nietzsche says about Christianity, unless God does really exist, and the man who hung on the cross was really the Son of God. And these things we can only believe in. Nietzsche rules out, and correctly so, all vagueness and half-hearted compromise, all evidences and arguments.

Nietzsche himself felt that arguments against Christianity were not too important either. He believed that Christianity had already been disposed of several times on that level. But he realized all too well that such easy conquests are worthless, since they arise from negation, from skepticism and relativism. They can become meaningful only if the opponent of Christianity himself takes a radical standpoint. Then Christianity becomes a matter of taste; and then there appears, in Nietzsche, the fight against Christianity, born from hatred, from the spirit of the Antichrist.

In the pages which follow, we shall see what standpoint Nietzsche took in his opposition to Christianity, how he came to adopt that particular standpoint, and how the bitterness of his fight against Christianity thus becomes understandable. Suffice it to say here that no one can really understand Nietzsche unless he goes back — as Nietzsche did — to essentials, to what lies behind his vexing treatment of Christianity; to the way he posed the religious problem, for it is from this that his charges against his greatest enemy grow.

Nietzsche understood well enough the strong strategic position of his opponent. The all-powerful "kingdom of the stupid" is not so stupid as it appears. We are the stupid, says Nietzsche, we who do not see that behind all this "hides God, who likes dark, crooked and wonderful ways, it is true, but who finally brings everything to a good end. It is ironic for those who thought that Christianity had been conquered by the natural sciences. For the Christian value-judgments were not at all conquered. 'Christ on the Cross' is the loftiest symbol — still. Jesus of Nazareth, the incarnated gospel of love, is seduction in its most awesome and irresistible form. Is there anything more seductive, more narcotic, more vicious, than the holy cross? And so clever a symbol. ' God on the cross'— don't you understand the terrible implication of this symbol? Everything that suffers, everything that hangs on the cross, is divine."

For Nietzsche, then, the cross of Christ is the beginning and the explanation of the *decadence* which gradually came over Europe. True, the error of the separation between spirit and body had already existed with the Greek, with Parmenides and especially with Plato; but it was Christianity, from the time of Paul on, which declared the body to be especially sinful, and which despised the body. And it was this contempt of the very things which life consists of, contempt of desires and passions, which led to the decline of culture in Europe.

There were various attempts to check this unholy development which followed the introduction of Christianity. The Renaissance was one such attempt. It was a liberation of man and his life-instincts. There were even Popes who were ashamed to be Christians. If only Caesar Borgia had become Pope, European culture might have retained some health. Nietzsche also admired Napoleon. But such truly free spirits did not know how to change the course Europe was following. Christianity was successful time after time in annihilating or crippling its enemies, those who witnessed to the power of life — the Roman Empire, Islam, the Renaissance.

The attack on Christianity by philosophy failed for other reasons. From Descartes on, philosophy was anti-Christian in its epistomology; but it was not anti-religious. So philosophy simply helped contribute to further decadence. And this was a continuous process. The seventeenth century was still aristocratic: orderly, strong-willed, and passionate: the century of reason. The eighteenth century was feminine, witty, superficial, libertine: the century of the heart. Then followed the nineteenth century; bestial, realistic, plebian; more honest, but weakwilled, sorrowful and fatalistic: the century of longing.

And with the nineteenth century European civilization arrived at the crossroads, the unmasking of the ideals of European culture. Men no longer believed in the immortality of the soul, or sin, or grace, or redemption, or any of the other ideas of Christianity. Ideals were shed like dead skin. From now on, says Nietzsche, there shall not be a religiously delimited world. It is indecent to be a Christian now, at this stage of civilization. *"And here begins my disgust."*

Disgust with what? Nietzsche says that for European civilization, Christianity has been unmasked and exposed as an illusion. And he is disgusted with those who have not wished this to happen. Priests and popes no longer err, he means; now they tell deliberate lies.

God is dead, God has died. Jasper correctly comments that Nietzsche does not say here that God does not exist, or that he does not believe in God; he is simply stating a fact in Western civilization. When Zarathustra leaves his solitude to walk among men, he encounters an old man, who says him to honor God in his song. Zarathustra laughs to himself as he leaves the old man, and remarks, "How is it possible! The old man . . . hasn 't heard the news, that God is dead."

Schubart thinks that Nietzsche sought God, and that in this question he came nearly as far as Dostoyevsky, who found God. This appears to me to be incorrect. It was self-evident to Nietzsche, and it helped set him on the way he chose to take, that God did not exist: and he felt it as a liberation from error that God had also died for his contemporaries.

According to Nietzsche, Christianity is to blame for the death of its God. For it was not life which was made divine in the God of Christianity, and the will was not declared to be holy. Christianity turned itself and its nihilistic life-denying morality against its own God, and finally became simply a denial of life, with its fictitious basis exposed. "Nihi*list* rhymes with Chr*ist:* and that isn't the only resemblance!"

Nihilism is implicit in the very nature of Christian morality, for decadent and nihilistic values appear wherever the will to power is lacking. The highest values, the life-affirming values, are then declared valueless. That is in a sense a positive thing, to declare a certain set of values non-existent. But the final result of two thousand years of blood-poisoning is a *passive* nihilism, a nihilism of decadence, the denial of the power of the spirit. Man stares into nothingness, he is tired, we are the men who are tired.

European man thus comes to stand before a terrible choice. Give up your worship (of God, morality, values, etc.) — or else give up *yourself.* The second is nihilism: but wouldn't the first also be nihilism? "That," says Nietzsche, "is *our* question." How could the first choice avoid ending in nihilism also? The positive emphasis in Nietzsche's philosophy circled this question tensely. The more Nietzsche concerned himself with this question, the more certain he became that the first choice would also carry him into nihilism, and that he was not only the prophet of the nihilism which whould dominate the coming century, but that he must also offer himself to nihilism, and become its priest as well.

V. NIHILISM

Before we follow Nietzsche's train of thought on this point any further, it is necessary to examine more closely the meaning of nihilism. What kind of "nothing" is meant here? Nietzsche describes nihilism in excellent fashion thus: "What does nihilism mean? *That the highest values are void.* That purpose vanishes. That the answer to 'why?' disappears." Nihilism thus means this, that nothing *holds;* that nothing binds me, no value, law, or norm; and that everything is *meaningless* and without sense. The term thus includes two different though closely related concepts: Nietzsche thus mentions them both in the same breath. For if there is a law, there is an indicator of direction, and then there is direction, and thus meaning. Or, on the other hand, if existence has meaning, it must emphasize relationship and order, and then law is implied, for the examination of existence is possible only in relation to a standard.

But if existence should be completely meaningless, if it yawns on the void of nothingness, then before that void all law would vanish, and the examination of existence would be impossible. And does not a nihilistic philosophy then become a self-contradictory idea? That is Nietzsche's problem.

It is noteworthy that both concepts named above, law and meaning, are central in a new Christian philosophy that has been developed at the Free University of Amsterdam by Herman Dooyeweerd * and Theo Vollenhoven. The idea of law, which a philosopher has, will determine his philosophy. Is law the law which God lets prevail, or is man the lawgiver, or is there a law without a lawgiver, or is there no law — we can see here how philosophies diverge from each other. The same holds true for meaning. Is meaning found in the existence of the existing, or in that the existent exists for the glory of God, or is it possible for something to exist which is so self-sufficient that it can exist without meaning, or is the meaning of existence found in humanity — or, is everything meaningless?

---

* Ed. note: Cf. H. Dooyeweerd, A *New Critique of Theoretical Thought,* Presbyterian and Reformed Publishing Co. (1953).

The series of alternatives above represent the Christian view of law and meaning, the secularized view, and finally the inevitable outcome of such a view, nihilism.

Jaspers says that nihilism is the result of being without *faith*. That is a valid enough characterization, if we look at the question from a human point of view. Faith can be defined as man's certainty of his relationship to that which for him is undoubtable: God, the law He gives, the destiny of life. This certainty can also exist if this faith is given to false gods. Or, faith can lose its guiding tenets and become merely an attitude, and then an inclination, and then a so-called open-mindedness ('so-called' since behind that open-mindedness there still exists the search for certainty, but it is sought in the believing man himself). It is only through a faith in, and certainty about, and relationship to one's own existence and perhaps also the existence of others, that 'open-mindedness' can give itself the appearance of being open-minded and free from belief. Jaspers supports this belief in open-mindedness, and sees it as a remedy for nihilism, which arises (he says) from the aftermath of dogmatic faith. What Jaspers does not understand is that it is rather this faith in open-mindedness which produces doubt (for with its vagueness about meaning and values, it logically excludes all certainty regarding existence); and then, for a courageous thinker, nihilism. It should be noted that this idea of transcendence (which Jaspers also calls God, and with which free existence joins itself through death) can easily be substituted by nothingness.

There is yet another characteristic of nihilism. *Sin* does not exist for the nihilist. Where there is no law, there can be no sin. And Nietzsche, consistently, explains the idea of sin as a mere fiction. He positively denies the existence of law or sin. And we might pause at this very point to consider how essential the difference is between Nietzsche, who positively believes in nihilism, and the man who drifts along in nihilism; between the man who seeks a way in nihilism, and the man who does not seek but who becomes dominated by nihilism; in short, between the *active* nihilist (such as Nietzsche) and the *passive* nihilist.

The latter type, which Nietzsche saw rising around him in Europe, is the *mass-man*, who can make no evaluations simply because he has no standards. This does not mean that the mass-man is free. On the contrary, he makes of himself a prison, fettered as he is by the superficial reality in which he lives, and by his own standard passions and caprices.

The mass-man simply drifts along in the stream of his environment. For him, everything is self-explanatory. He does not question anything which exists; for questions cannot be asked when there is no law. Facts, *that which exists*, have taken over the role of law. "To exist" becomes synonymous with "to be a value." This short circuiting with practice, this restriction to the pragmatic, makes the mass-man extremely short-sighted. The trivial events of the day dominate his life. He has no perspective. He knows only an eternal present; for him, the past is empty, and the future an opaque mystery.

The mass-man can still act, to some extent. But his actions have no goals; he acts not to "put his hand to the plow," but simply to give event to his displeasures. And he is displeased whenever events are contrary — not contrary to what he thinks is right, for he has no such standards, but rather contrary to his uncontrolled desires. That is his second "tyrant." The first tyrant rules him with the "law" that whatever exists has no need of explanation; the second with the "law" of egotism. Both make him impossible to contact, for discussion and appeal become possible only through that objectivity gained in relation to an objective law.

If these two masters of the mass-man are in harmony, he goes along without any trouble. But if not (and this is generally a collective experience), then tension develops, caused by his dissatisfaction. But this does not move the mass-man to true action, for true action is possible only if standards of value have been established.[1]

And yet the mass-man does exert a good deal of indirect influence, for the course of events, and those that direct it, are concerned about his desires and wishes, and endeavor to restore peace. And this influence thus initiates in society a drift towards *decadence*. The law of sin prevails, for if life is directed simply toward pleasure, it seeks out the lowest forms of pleasure. Life decays more and more, for the voice of the law is silent, and the brake of conscience shattered. This can be seen clearly in the disappearance of all notions of guilt and shame, a tendency which is very evident in contemporary plays, novels, and conversations. The alarming thing about all this is that it is *not* the outgrowth of a dynamic life of passion, but due rather to the development of a cold, matter-of-fact outlook, which mixes good

---

[1] In actual fact, of course, such an extreme form of the mass-man is never encountered. What is noticeable in modern man is rather the increasing dominance of such characteristics. The completely consistent mass-man is as impossible as a completely consistent nihilism is untenable. Hence as soon as the principle of lawlessness nears its complete expression, with the mass-man and the man of power, the period of great destruction will begin, and the final judgment will be at hand.

and bad, right and wrong, beautiful and ugly, into a completely homogeneous compound. This decadence is not typified in the fact that sin reveals itself, but rather in the fact that there is no longer any comprehension of what sin is.

It might be objected that such a development is unlikely to take place, for sin is ugly and repellent; that it would tend to check this descent into chaos and anarchy by its very ugliness, which would become more and more apparant as sin increasingly revealed itself. It might be replied, however, that this decay, in the first place, is gradual and almost unnoticeable. And even more importantly, the ugly actuality of sin is hidden, during this process of decay, by a beautiful camouflage. This is a covering which masks the ugly reality with a mantle of love, righteousness, beauty, courage, and so forth. A deceptive covering which makes the future appear as a thing of alluring happiness, a sweet mystery, an exciting event; and the future after the immediate future yet more sweet, sublime, and exciting, until finally, as this internal decadence spreads and flourishes beneath the misleading exterior of progress, there remains only a disconsolate ruin in which no more hope is possible. To be sure, history might inform us of some of this beforehand; but let us not forget it was the great historian Huizinga who thought that this deceptive covering of sham and illusion is today greater than ever before.

These remarks do not contradict what has been said before. It is not so much that *sin* is camouflaged, for the mass-man has no apprehension of sin; but rather that whatever stands in the way of the mass-man's desires is concealed under a false exterior. Everything must *appear* to help satisfy his desires.

It is striking how superficial and fleeting this disguise usually is. It is easy to see through the fraud and the enervation of this decadence, which must be camouflaged by advertising, political slogans, solemn speeches, films, summer resorts, dancing, parties, sports, and so forth. But the modern man is so impatient and covetous, so amiable and superficial, so uncritical and forgetful, that it does not take much to drive him on "as an ox to the slaugther."

Well, to what extent does Nietzsche's evaluation of modernity coincide with the Christian evaluation of it? They agree on this, that modern civilization is decadent, that it has lost its élan. And they agree on this, that this decadence, as history shows, is inevitable. And on this, that this decadence expressed itself most fully in passive nihilism, in which the values that have previously held good become worthless.

But the two evalutions differ radically on the interpretation of this data, and over the future which may follow it. Nietzsche contends that moral values actually *are* worthless, so that now pretense has finally been divorced from reality, that pretense for which humanity for thousands of years has suffered the floggings of conscience. The Christian, on the contrary, says that God does exist, and that His law is valid, and that whenever society loses touch with this law, it turns to the pretense or illusion that only life has value, and this sets it on the road to decadence.

Nietzsche rejoices that the pretense and illusion of the Christian faith was followed first by the philosophical separation of values from religious faith (which ended the need for God), and then by the exposure of all values as pretense. The Christian, on the contrary, would put the emphasis like this: the philosophical separation of values from faith separated values and norms from Him who established them and preserved them; and this not only immediately weakened the binding validity of morals, but also changed them from true values (based on God) to false values (based on reason). It then was only a matter of time before the falseness and pretense of these values (now separated from God) were exposed. And indeed, this exposure has been the main achievement of subjective philosophy during the past four centuries.

The problem of appearance and reality, pretense and actuality, has always played an important role in philosophy. This is due to the fact that philosophy here becomes concerned with its religious foundations. In Nietzsche's philosophy, this problem produces a dramatic tension. Hence it might be desirable, especially for the understanding of philosophy, to inquire more closely how Nietzsche, who accepted the conclusions of modern philosophy, was thereby bound to draw the logical consequence: nihilism. We can well learn from this examination the closeness of the connection between the development of an ideology, a view of life, and philosophy. For it is not a case of Nietzsche's simply accommodating his philosophy to his outlook on life; no, he felt driven not only by the spirit of his age but also by the inner dialectic of modern philosophy, to nihilism.

VI. PHILOSOPHY ON ITS WAY TOWARDS NIHILISM

It is not true, despite common belief, that the Reformation produced a view of life which extinguished the light of reason and replaced it by the irrationality of faith. Remember rather, for example, the convincing power with which Calvin used reason in his *Institutes*. No, what men of the Reformation stood for was this, that religious faith was the beginning and basis of reason, and a boundary line which marked the limits of reason.

In humanistic philosophy, on the other hand, this view of faith as the basis and limit of reason was denied, since the humanists did not want the sovereignty of reason to be limited. The humanist philosophers attempted to understand and justify the values which they wished to hold good, but this attempt was made within the framework of reason. Religious faith was no longer accepted as a thing which could give certainty to values.

This weakened Christianity as well as values. Slowly but surely the authority of faith was limited to an ever decreasing area, and the evidence of things not seen was more and more replaced by the evidence of things men claimed to see by the light of reason. Rationalism became dominant. Men still had a way which led to God, but it was a rational way, and at its end stood merely a rationally apprehendable idea which men chose to call God. Honoring God thus became in actuality simply honoring divine Reason, and thus honoring man himself.

The values which humanistic philosophy honored, and the morality which it prescribed, were still related to Christian values and morality. And this could hardly have been otherwise. Not only was humanism related to a Christian society still, and indeed had *developed* from the decaying Christian society of the late Middle Ages, but even more important, every positive element in humanism could be nothing else than a residue of the true values established by God. For there is no other positive law for life besides God's law.

What weakened the validity of humanistic values in the long run was humanism's failure to retain an objective lawgiver. It became steadily clearer that it was man himself who discovered values and who decided what values should be judged valid. And the more these values simply became constructs of human reason, the vaguer they became adulterated. Though the same words might be used, they took on a secularized meaning, characterized by the assumption that man rather than God was the sole criterion and judge of values. (The same process can be seen today in the changing meaning of such words as justice, love, comradeship, freedom, personality, etc.) This process is what we would call the transition from *real* values to *fictitious* values, from reality to pretense.

And with man now established as the new lawgiver, the laws and values themselves began to fade away. This was a slow process, spread over centuries, but it was inevitable and unmistakable. (Inevitable because the man who leaves God and will not live by the grace of Christ is delivered over to sin.) A kind of mutual adaptation arose; man adapted himself to social practice, and social practice adapted itself to man, and in this mutual adaptation both of them decayed. The values of humanism, those values for which man was the only criterion and judge, gradually molded away.

This development took place against a background of a kind of faith, faith in man as his own savior — for the idea of sovereign reason could never dispense with some kind of faith, and indeed it grew out of a faith, the faith in reason. This faith endured until the increasingly evident failure of man to save himself made it untenable; that is, until it became impossible to ignore any longer the result of this decadence, the escape of sin from the bonds which had fettered it. Whether or not this was called "sin" is irrelevant here; the point is that the reality of the release of sinful forces into social life was not only recognized but even regarded as a decisive fact. Sin — whether it was called the struggle for life, the struggle for existence, the struggle for success, the struggle of the classes — was stressed in the writings of men like Adam Smith, Charles Darwin, and Karl Marx, and it came to be an important and often dominant preoccupation of the modern outlook on life.

Before things had reached that point, however, philosophy had already taken a new tack. The constructs of reason in the field of morality, norms, ideals, etc., became so abstract and speculative, especially in the idealistic philosophers, that most philosophers rejected reason at the basis of philosophy. They turned their backs on the view that reason could furnish that certainty which was necessary. They looked for certainty not in reason, but in *experience,* or in the facts. There exists no certainty except in that which can be sensed and controlled. It is not difficult to see how important this new tack was for the idea of real objective values, and thus also for any notion of freedom and responsibility. It became impossible to hold these ideas, and the objectivity of values was given up; from this new standpoint, man could find out what he should do only from social practice, the actual practice of society.

In other words, the difference between values and facts vanished; there was no longer any room for a demand that men obey objective values; and the problem of sin, which had still retained a place (though an abstract place) in idealism, was no longer regarded as a problem — for sin can be seen as a problem only if a difference between values and facts is retained. It is perhaps unnecessary to add that there remained no trace of even the watered-down God of idealism in the positive environment, the "facts" available to the senses, from which the positivists constructed their new philosophy. Oh, true enough, men could still believe in God if they wished; but this was a personal belief, a kind of eccentricity; and science, almighty science, was busy limiting and relativizing even this area of private belief, with a good deal more success than reason had formerly had. The kernel of atheism is clearly visible in positivism.

The same thing happened to objective values. While society did not follow immediately what the scholars taught, and while "positive" *Wissenschaft* still furnished a miscellaneous assortment of certainties, positivism had no real defense against the complete historicizing and subjectivizing of values; no real defense against the notion that what holds today does not hold tomorrow, and what holds for one man has no meaning for another; no defense, that is, against nihilism, which is the lack of any general objective values. And so, when society had reached this stage of decay, it was only necessary for some scholar to draw this logical consequence from the idea that experience furnished the only certainty. It was Nietzsche who adopted the position of nihilism, both for philosophy and for life.

Before this position could be reached from positivism, however, it was necessary that one of the bulwarks of positivism — science — be undermined. For positivism sought certainty not only in experience but also in science. It was the instrument which men could use to map out all of "positive" experience, in order to control social practice. Men needed only to discover the laws (not moral laws, but physical laws) which governed this experience, this world of facts, and then through the use of generalization he would be able to work out a comprehensive and descriptive science which would take in all of nature and culture. But this system, too, was speculative, and it too became more and more divorced from real life. Men began to see that science was incapable of disclosing essential truth. It appeared as — though science was stripping from reality all of its important characteristics — continuity, individuality, freedom, and so forth.

In order to solve this problem, philosophy adopted a very subtle and dangerous method, that of pragmatism. According to this new position, the task of *Wissenschaft* of science and scholarship, was not to discover truth. *Wissenschaft* was simply an instrument which man used to maintain social practices and to help realize his practical goals. The question of whether science was true or not was completely unimportant, unless it somehow affected the question of whether it was useful. That was the decisive factor, and if anyone still wanted to use the term "truth," he could say that whatever was useful was true. And indeed. this conclusion had already been implicit in the basic ideas of positivism, for there the norms of truth were based on experience only. This consequence of positivism, potentially destructive of philosophy and science both, was fully developed only later, however, especially by Nietzsche.

When closely examined, pragmatism turns out to be a philosophical nihilism, a nihilistic denial of objective truth. Though pragmatism must be carefully distinguished from a nihilism which denied all values and denied that reality had meaning, this latter form was nevertheless implicit in pragmatism. The old positivism had defended itself against philosophical nihilism with the speculative idea of an all embracing science — though experience gives no certainty at all about this. And likewise pragmatism (for example, American pragmatism), though it gave up all objective values, defended itself against complete nihilism with the speculative idea of continual progress — though experience can give us no certainty about this either.

Thus for a philosophy which took its positivistic starting point seriously, there remained nothing which could vouch for its certainty except the subjective and fleeting experience of the individual philosopher. And the positivistic philosopher can escape this fearful narrowing of his outlook only by indulging in the very sort of speculative thinking which is condemned by his own positivism.

Thought has no values and no meaning: existence has no values and no meaning. That is the position Nietzsche agreed with, and the position on which he sought a basis for a philosophy.

VII. THE PHILOSOPHER OF NIHILISM

Nietzsche was deeply convinced of the inevitability of the succession of phases through which humanistic philosophy had passed. Anyone who gave up the certainty of religious faith, he thought, must also give up those illusionary certainties which subjective philosophy had held so previous to Nietzsche. He knew that the way back through these successive phases was closed for him. And so we encounter in his writings the philosophical tendencies we have been describing.

The philosopher can find certainty only in experience, said Nietzsche. "Even the great spirits have only their hands-width of *experience*. It is precisely when they go beyond experience that their windy expansiveness and their stupidity begin." We cannot see around a corner, and ungrounded speculation will not help us to do so. Nietzsche wants to ignore all questions and all supposed reality which cannot be tested by experiment. Therefore he approves of positivism, which realized that the categories of reason were not only underivable from experience, but even contrary to experience.

And experience also denies all the values of science, says Nietzsche. Experience teaches us that what is called the truth of science is simply a fiction. Scientists ask only those questions which they know they can answer. He finds it unacceptable to base certainty and the truth of science on so small an area of human life as human consciousness. For what is consciousness? It functions only so long as and insofar as it is useful. "Everything of which we can be conscious is thoroughly over-simplified, schematized, pre-prepared, arranged on display." This over-simplification may work to our advantage, but it has nothing to do with truth. "He is a thinker: that means he lets himself conclude that things are simpler than they actually are." Sometimes Nietzsche goes even further with his pragmatic interpretation: "In the final analysis, man discovers in things nothing more than he has previously put into them. This re-discovery is called science; and what we impose on the facts . . . . is called art, religion, love, pride." The over-simplified interpretations of reality which are awakened by our wishes become, due to our intellectual indolence, solidified into convictions.

It should be understood that with such an outlook the question of truth or falsity recedes into the background. Truth and falsity can both be useful. Man's intellect has often produced erroneous views during the course of history; what Nietzsche finds important is that some of these erroneous views have been useful in helping to preserve humanity.

So far we have considered the results of science and scholarship, of *Wissenschaft*. Nietzsche concludes that whether or not real truth does exist, it is certain that *Wissenschaft* cannot teach us how to find it. Or, in other words, the tree of life is different from the tree of knowledge.

The question now becomes this, whether or not Nietzsche believed that real *truth* did exist. There are many places, many citations, where he seems to answer both yes and no to this question. But that is, after all, understandable. For Nietzsche is involved in an insoluble dilemma. Truth can exist only in connection with an objective law. But for Nietzsche it is only experience, his experience, that is valid; there is no objective law; and hence there can be no truth. And yet, whoever takes such a conclusion seriously can logically do nothing but remain silent; indeed, he must refuse to think; for no matter how many problems come up, or how many erroneous opinions prevail, when we deny that truth exists it becomes ridiculous to begin thinking, to commence searching.... for truth! Nietzsche did not keep silent; he tells us what truth means for him, though his message is often camouflaged by paradoxes. He has wrestled with truth. No matter what he says, he cannot really be a complete nihilist in the philosophical sense, for no one can. After all, what does "useful" mean? That involves a question of truth, really. And when Nietzsche supports an idea of destiny, he is establishing an orderliness in experience which no one who denies the existence of truth can logically support.

There is no way for him to escape from the blind alley in which he had placed himself, no way he could reach truth. In the first place, historical relativism barred the way. How ridiculous, thought Nietzsche, to seek a truth which would be valid for all periods and all times. What a prejudice is shown when scholars assume that we know more today than has ever been known before. There are no absolute truths, for there are no eternal facts. Indeed, it is impossible for anyone who regards experience and facts as the only certainties to bridge the gap separating the experience of our historical period and the experience of any other historical period.

And the nature of experience raises another and even more formidable barrier against the attempt to find certain truth. For there is no way to bridge the gap between my experience and someone else's experience. And Nietzsche accepted this consequence of a subjective view of truth. "I believe that everyone must have his own interpretation of everything that can be interpreted, since every man is a unique thing that takes a completely new and unsharable attitude toward all other things." It is man's indolence which makes him leave this uniqueness and seek commonness. We must express truth, said Fichte, even if the world goes to pieces because of it. Yes, says Nietzsche, but we must first have it. What Fichte means, he continues, is that everyone must express his own interpretation, even if everything else goes by the board; and this can be discussed.

Every philosopher has in fact loved *his own* truth, says Nietzsche. The future philosopher wil not conceal that fact as previous philosophers have. "Finally, things must be as they are and have been: great things are reserved for the great, abysses for the profound, tenderness and shudder for the tender-minded — in short, everything rare for the rare ones." Man possesses in his knowledge nothing more than his own biography. And here is the origin of Nietzsche's view that facts do not exist as such; there are only interpretations of facts. Elsewhere he says: "*My basic law: there are no ethical phenomena; only an ethical interpretation of phenomena. And this interpretation is of non-ethical origin."*

Nietzsche realized full well where this train of thought would lead him: to complete solitude. "The higher type of philosophical man surrounds himself with solitude, not because he likes to be alone, but because he is something which has no counterpart." He calls on his readers: "Be a man, and do not follow me, but — yourself." He does not want to found a religion, and whenever he meets religious people he has to wash his hands afterwards. "I do not want "believers," I think that I am too ill-natured to believe in myself, and I never speak to the masses. Yet I am terrified that one fine day people will make a saint out of me.... I don't want to be a saint; I'd much rather be a clown.... Perhaps I am a clown.... And nevertheless or rather *not* nevertheless — for there has never been a worse liar than the saint — I speak the truth. My truth is a *terrible* truth for men formerly called *lies* truth."

Nietzsche saw no chance, philosophically speaking, to reach out beyond his own limited personal experience. For in order to do that, he would need an objective basis, a religious certainty, and where could he find such a thing? And yet he felt that he must reach out, for within the realm of his own limited experience there was only solitude and silence; nihilism and nothingness ruled that realm. But he could find no means to bridge the gap which would not be illusion and pretense. So, like a frantic prisoner, he shakes the bars of his cell, trying to escape from nihilism. No: say rather trying to preserve nihilism and find a justification for it.

He recognized no truth — but yet he did recognize a truth, his own, a terrible truth. He wanted no disciples — but he wrote book after book to win converts to his ideas. And so he oscillates between the two poles of doubt and belief; the first always haunted him, and he never could find a means to reach the second.

He thought that he stood at the gateway to a new development. The great adventure of the first true philosophy could now begin. "We philosophers and free spirits feel when we hear the news that 'the old God is dead,' as if we stand at a new dawn; our hearts overflow with thankfulness, astonishment, surmise and expectation.... we can finally set sail again with our ships....the sea, *our* sea, again lies open; perhaps there never has been such an open sea."

Yes, Nietzsche exposed much pretense and many illusions; but he had nothing left over for himself. His own ideas of reality and truth could never take clear form. His judgments collapse almost as soon as they are formed, because of the strength of his tendency towards centrifugal thinking. As Brugmans remarks, the reading of Nietzsche hence becomes something of a nightmare. The reader rushes happily to one of Nietzsche's books: he will encounter someone whom he knows well. But then he shrinks back from the indifferent and even inimical visage which jeeringly faces him.

This is truly a perplexing situation. Nietzsche must have something to hold fast to, some certainty. Well, it can be found in that which thrusts itself upon him from his own experience: Life, passionate, wayward instinctive life, his life. But can we find certainty there, and if so, on what grounds? What men call justice and goodness is only a relationship between instincts, Nietzsche had said; so he still hasn't gotten anywhere; he must go further, he must find something which can give direction and purpose to life. "The thinker: that today is someone in whom the instinct to truth fights its first battles with the errors which stifle life, after the instinct to truth has also revealed itself as a force which stifles life. The feeling for truth must justify itself before another forum: as a means for the preservation of humanity."

But why preserve humanity? Man is so completely unimportant. What does the preservation of life have to do with truth? How can we be sure that a realm of wills and goals actually exists? Isn't it all simply a realm of chance and stupidity?

"The iron hands of destiny, which shake the dice-box of chance, play their endless game." "*Perhaps* our act of will, our goals, are exactly such casts of the dice." Man becomes a comic figure when he imagines that he himself is the chief goal of the universe, and preens himself on his cosmic mission. "If a God did create the world, then he created man as his court jester, as a source of eternal amusement." The animals must see man as a being like themselves, who has lost his healthy animal outlook; as an absurd, laughing, weeping, unlucky animal.

So what is there to philosophize about? Look at the butterfly, winging his carefree way over the sea-cliffs, where grow the flowers he likes. He does not fret and worry about the fact that he lives only for a day, and that the night will be too cold for him. Perhaps, says Nietzsche, perhaps that is my philosophy. But Nietzsche also sees himself as a bird winging his way purposefully over the boundless ocean, mapping a road for others to follow. A path; but what path, where to? Shall it be our fate to become stranded on that question?

Nietzsche can give no answer except a "perhaps." A hazardous perhaps. The philosopher, he says, must be an artist. That may prove to be, he suspects, a way out of our impasse, out of this void. *Art* is more godlike than truth. And in addition, philosophy must be *action*. But what kind of action, directed to what end? "It is better to will nothing than not to will at all." But still, what kind of action should we take? God is dead, and man is an animal whose animal instincts cannot give us a direction or goal, and outside of man there is nothing. And yet the inspiration to action must come from something outside the individual man; only in that way can passive nihilism be transformed to active. And it is exactly here that Nietzsche resorts to *myth*, which plays such an important role in his philosophy.

We have moved, in the discussion above, from the problems of philosophical nihilism to the problems of nihilism as an ideology, an outlook on life — and we hardly noticed the transition. Nietzsche too makes no sharp separation between the two things. Philosophy forces him to the position of denying the existence of knowledge and truth; and the decadence of life confronts him with another facet of the same nothingness, the denial that meaning exists.

VIII. THE HIGH PRIEST OF NIHILISM

Nietzsche begins his book *The Will To Power* with the remark that he is the first completely nihilistic European, but one who nevertheless has already lived through nihilism — one who had it behind him, under him, around him.

Where did Nietzsche finally arrive? Did the bird finally reach land? Did his sacrifice make sense? Did a light appear to him in the darkness of nothingness? Vloemans wants us to believe just that. Nietzsche was certainly not a nihilist, he says. He has seen a new dawn, and pointed the way to the land of the future.

Vloemans' wish is father to his thought; his wish that there will be a meaningful future, but without God and without Christ. That was also Nietzsche's hope. He meant by his remark in *The Will To Power* that nihilism is not enough, that there must be a counter-movement away from nothingness. New values are needed. But such remarks and Nietzsche's attempts to reach the other shore of the ocean of nothingness, which we are about to examine, show only this: that nihilism is indefensible and untenable. What he tried to do shows that he rebelled against nihilism, but not that he escaped from it. Nietzsche realized this full well. He knew that he was fundamentally a nihilist. What he hoped to do was to rise above decadence and passive nihilism. But how is it possible to find a way to action, in nihilism? That was his problem: to develop an *active nihilism* as a sign of the heightened power of the spirit. And he does not leave the reader in doubt about his meaning. Nihilism, he says, is not only the contemplation of nothingness, the belief that everything is going to wrack and ruin; it is also this, that man has to direct his movement.

It is at this point, the giving of *meaning* to reality, that nihilism undergoes its greatest tensions, religious tensions. Objectivity is given up; the man Nietzsche himself is at stake. Nietzsche annihilates everything, including himself, and yet seeks an escape from the meaninglessness of annihilation, and hopes that a new dawn will somehow break. He wrote to Rohde that he reckoned himself among the most thorough nihilists, "although I do not for a moment doubt that I will find a way out, the opening through which one can reach a 'something.'"

Nietzsche wants the stream of civilization, now at its lowest point, emptying itself in nihilism, to change direction; and in so doing to save civilization even in this eleventh hour. And he pins his hopes on a dynamic acceptance of life. *Life* is his basic motif. It alone is without pretense. And the joyous acceptance of life, instead of the denial and abuse of life which has hitherto prevailed, will bring about a new future.

But is there anything which can direct this life besides the whims of its desires and dislikes, its passions and hates? So seen, life in itself has no meaning, and can be called neither active nor passive. There is no possible way to tie it in with decadence or with a revival of culture.

It can be said that life is destiny, and regularly Nietzsche does say that. But then he is saying something more than what is furnished by experience. And furthermore, once that has been said, there is nothing more that can be said in clarification.

When Nietzsche feels that he must distinguish between a Yes and a No to life, between a rejection and affirmation of life, he has already slipped into a way of thinking which by his own standards must be rejected as speculative. But — that is the only way out of the impasse.

Nietzsche seeks a way out by turning from the life of the individual to the life of the human race. This can perhaps furnish a goal which cannot be found in the life of the individual. Hence, says Nietzsche, the goal of individual life is not to annihilate itself; the individual must help the human race. The individual by himself means nothing. Pain and desire are forces which must be used to preserve the human race. If the individual can no longer be of any use to humanity, he should end his life.

The position of Nietzsche thus drives him from one extreme to the other; it is noteworthy that this development in his thought is closely paralleled by the similar change from individualism to collectivism in European society.

But does the preservation of the human species really furnish Nietzsche with a goal, a way out of his dilemma? Can it give meaning to culture, can it give culture a direction along which to move?

Not at all! And thus Nietzsche must take a further step. It is not the mere preservation of the human species, but the fostering and development of a *higher* species which gives direction and meaning to culture. And since life is conflict, this must be a development through conflict. Hence there must be at least one basic contrast in society: and that, says Nietzsche, is the contrast between the aristocrats, the *masters,* and the crowd, the *herd.* Every higher culture or civilization has two types of men: those who work and those who do not: or, more accurately, those who work because they have to, and those who work voluntarily. Anyone who does not have at least two thirds of the day free for his own interests is a slave, a member of the herd. The characteristic of the master is that he is free, he recognizes no law, he despises authority. He goes his own way; the herd serves simply to satisfy his love of conflict. These noble beasts of prey can be found in all higher civilizations.

In his treatment of this theme also, Nietzsche takes a position which is the complete opposite of the Christian view.

The differentiation of society into masters and herd-men serves Nietzsche as a basis for his outlook on the future of our civilization. He is constantly concerned over the problem of ending the decadence of our culture. Well, in the course of the cultural development of the masters, there must emerge a *"super-man,"* a higher race. "Not humanity, but superman, is the goal."

First of all, the tide of democracy must be halted and driven back. Wars can be a further means of halting the decadence of our civilization, and Nietzsche actually saw the beginning of an age of wars.

Shall the superman emerge? Man has possibilities; he has not yet become fixed in a merely animal status; and although thus undecided he appears to be a cancerous growth on the earth, he also has the possibility of becoming the superman — the human who uses lies, power, and egotism as instruments; a demonic being. He is a centaur — half animal and half man — with angel's wings. He is the barbarian from heaven, he dances over the abyss. He is the creating law-giver, man fully realized, the meaning of this world.

Nietzsche seeks a way out. For him, God is dead, and nothing remains but *life.* He loves life, but he also hates it, for it is the enemy who threatens him with meaninglessness. Life is changeable and uncontrolled; like a mischievous woman, he says in the *Dance-Song of Zarathustra*. Life is a wild, matchless wisdom. And yet as he abandons himself to it, doubt creeps in: "What! Are you still alive, Zarathustra? Why? What for? Through what? Where to? Where? How? Is it not absurd to remain alive?"

He sought the carefree absurdity of the dance of life in vain, though he wished it passionately, for the restlessness of his spirit robbed him of all joy.

So he feels like a drowning man with no handhold. He will free himself from this mischievous woman by believing in man, and give perspective to this meaningless life by the superman — but as he reaches for the superman to escape from the animal, the wild wisdom of life laughs at him; and if he listen to its siren call, he can find nothing to give meaning to life. Zarathustra sees an acrobat balancing on his tight rope high above the crowd, and he says: "Man is a tight rope, stretched between animal and superman. A tight rope above an abyss. A dangerous journey to the other side, danger beneath, danger behind, and danger to stand still. What gives greatness to man is that he is not a goal but a bridge. What is reprehensible in man is that he is a transition and a going under."

Does Nietzsche actually believe that the superman will appear, and that the superman can escape being meaningless? We need not expect a clear and unequivocal answer to such questions from Nietzsche. He does make such statements as this: "The hidden *yes* in you is stronger than every 'no' or 'perhaps,' those things from which you and your age are sick. And if you go to sea you emigrants, you will be driven that way — by faith." Nietzsche knew how much was at stake in his age. In this decadent civilization, man could again sink to the level of the ape. Lubac paraphrases Nietzsche's problem thus: "Shall we rediscover a myth which can save us, or shall we disappear in a catastrophe? The question is essential. It has the compelling quality of Hamlet's dilemma: to be or not to be."

But how can he speak of faith here, this man who fought so bitterly against all speculation? Does he have, after all, does he have any reasoned arguments which can give a natural perspective more certainty than the supernatural perspective which he scoffingly exposed as pretense and sham? For the superman is really a *myth*, a myth which must arouse our civilization from its decadence and passivity. "Without a myth, every culture loses its healthy and creative natural powers."

To understand what this myth actually meant for Nietzsche, to penetrate into his spiritual viewpoint, is difficult for anyone who has an unshakeable religious faith, and who is therefore free from the shackles of purely positivistic experience. It is certainly not correct to say that he found in this myth a resting point, a point of balance. He was under too much pressure: from his need for belief, on the one hand, and his doubts of any certainty not based on positive experience on the other. How could it be otherwise? For Nietzsche, although deeply convinced that only a rock-firm faith could overcome the decadence of Europe, was too honest to pretend that such a faith would be anything more than a speculation for him. And hence his writings swing from one extreme to the other. And behind these writings is a spirit which could finally resolve this conflict only by shattering itself.

Who is the superman, what is it like? It seems to me that Nietzsche did not concern himself too much with this question; and yet it is of great importance for his thought, since for him everything depends on the active-nihilistic superman. Even if we examine what Nietzsche says about him, the superman never takes on clear form. Zarathustra, who is both the prophet and type of the superman, remains a vague figure, always discoursing and arguing — though according to Nietzsche, it is *action* rather than such speechmaking which will characterize the superman. Nietzsche gradually abandons using the great figures of history as analogies. Once he understands them, he becomes disgusted with them: "I have never yet met a great man."

Besides this vaguesness, there is another problem which finally drove Nietzsche on to yet another theme. The problem is this: how does the superman mean anything, and once he has come, what will follow him? Once Nietzsche realized the implication of this question, he realized also that he was in danger of resorting to pretense and sham; and to avoid this, he had the courage to take on a still heavier burden, the meaninglessness of the *eternal recurrence* of all things. When Vloemans says that Nietzsche contradicts himself with this new idea, he only shows that he lacks the courage to follow Nietzsche into the darkness of nihilism.

This is not a new idea: the theme of eternal recurrence occurs in many ancient philosophies. But with Nietzsche, this idea is born from the unbearable tensions of nihilism. He sets it over against the naive modern idea of continual progress, and also over against the future Kingdom of Heaven of Christianity.

It is a spine-chilling idea, an idea which struck Nietzsche like a bolt of lightning, and he wrestled and struggled to go along with it, to like it, to like this prospect of eternity. "Suppose that on a certain day or night a demon hunted you out in your most solitary solitude and said: 'This Life, as you now live it and have lived it, must be lived again, and yet uncountable times; there shall be nothing new in it, ... The eternal hourglass of existence will be turned over again and again, and you with it, a grain of sand." Would you not throw yourself on earth and gnashing your teeth. curse such a demon? Or have you once enjoyed a moment in your life so magnificent that you would answer, 'You are a god, and I have never heard anything more divine?' And as this thought of the demon exerted its power over you, you would change your present life, or perhaps even shatter it; and the question which would arise would always be, 'would you want to do this over and over and over again, countless times?' — that question would have the weightiest influence on your actions. How would you reconcile with yourself and with your life so that you would long for nothing more than this last eternal seal and stamp?"

Nietzsche's idea of eternal recurrence, it may be noted, is not wholly respectable in any scholarly sense. It might be noted also that in accepting this idea, Nietzsche is turning to a mechanistic type of thought which is usually foreign to him. But this idea must be seen as Nietzsche's alternative to God, now that God is dead, and his remedy for the senselessness of life. It is a medicine which can work only if men learn to love destiny, particularly the destiny of eternal recurrence. Men must have desire through all eternity. "Anguish says: perish. But every desire wills eternity — deep, deep eternity." "Was this — life? By the will of Zarathustra: well now! Once again!"

It is very understandable that Nietzsche repeatedly sought refuge in the attitude towards life expressed in play. For play offered — and not only to him — a way out from the perplexity of unsolved questions of meaning. "The matureness of man: that is the rediscovery of the seriousness of play, which he knew as a child."

Perhaps it is unnecessary to show in detail that neither the life without values, nor the myth of the superman which had no meaning, nor the destiny of eternal recurrence, could give Nietzsche a point of rest, a central point. Though he rejoiced whenever he was able to develop one of these concepts and put it into writing, his joy was not real, for each concept destroyed the previous one, and each of them was untenable by itself. Finally Nietzsche thought he would be able to unite them under one basic concept, a principle which drove creative life towards the superman, which placed the masters over against the herd, and which regulated the eternal recurrence: *the will to power.* "I distinguished the active power, the creative force in the midst of chance." That is the demon which rules men. "Not poverty, not desire — no, the love power is the demon of men. Give them everything, food, health, a dwelling, amusement — they are and remain unhappy and capricious, for the demon waits and waits, and wants to be satisfied." Happiness is the feel of power. Goodness is whatever results from power. The will to power rules every change. There is no free will in this will to power; one can distinguish only the weak will and the strong will.

At the conclusion of his book *The Will To Power*, Nietzsche gives us an insight into the synthesis he meant to build. "The world: a monster of power, without beginning, without end, fixed, metal, a whole of power, which becomes neither larger nor smaller.... closed in by 'nothing' as by a boundary.... as a game of power and ways of power, at the same time one and many .... a sea of storming and flowing energies, eternally changing, eternally running back in the terrible years of recurrence, with an ebb tide and flood tide of forms, ranging from the simplest to the most complex, from the stillest, stiffest, coldest to the most radiant, the wildest; contradicting itself and then turning again from complexity to simplicity, from the game of contradiction to the desire for harmony.... blessing itself as that which must eternally return, as a becoming which never becomes satisfied, which knows not satiety nor tiredness — my *Dionysian* world which eternally creates itself and eternally annihilates itself, this world of secrets of double pleasure, this world *Beyond Good and Evil* with no goal, just as there can be no goal in the happiness of a circle without will, just as no ring can have good will towards itself — this world, do you want a *name* for this world? A *solution* for all its riddles?.... *This world is the will to power — and nothing more.* And you yourself are this will to power — and nothing more."

That this will is not free; that this infinity of circular processes is a speculation; that it is difficult to see how man, driven by these processes, can ever move forward, or how he can desire such processes — all this only emphasizes that nihilism, no matter what motif it takes up to save itself — can end only in a decadent ruin. But the most important thing is that Nietzsche did find in his last motif a cultural principle which would be followed in actual practice. He expected that it would bring victory over decadence and passive nihilism. We have seen this "victory" in our present century. It is the worship of power, the value-less activism, always restless, driven by the fear of meaninglessness, and finally pouring itself out in annihilation and self-annihilation.

Nietzsche could find no point of rest, no basis for his thought. His ideas oscillated between two opposing poles. Doubt and belief, butterfly and bird, sun and darkness, dance and action, destiny and will, play and culture — he could never reconcile them with each other. The more he neared the boundaries of nothingness, the more irreconcilable everything appeared. And Nietzsche thus became steadily more conscious of the most radical antithesis: that between *Christ on the Cross* and his ideal of man, the *Dionysian nihilistic man of power*. He rejected every synthesis and every compromise. He realized that only the *Antichrist* could be put up in real opposition to Christ. And he wanted to create the Antichrist, he wanted to be the Antichrist. His great question, and he found no answer to it, was whether the Antichrist could obtain stature and permanence as the antipode of the Crucified One. He was so filled with this antithesis, and so much in a quandary over it, that during the period of his insanity he wrote the two names over and over on scraps of paper — Dionysius and the Crucified.

Did he see his arch-enemy, Christ, accurately? Certainly not. We might pause here a moment in order to make clear why Nietzsche misinterpreted Christ so completely, and what it was in him that he fought so bitterly.

Nietzsche distinguished very sharply between Christ and Christianity. It is almost as if he wanted to protect the Crucified One against Christianity. "The word 'Christianity' is already a misunderstanding — there was fundamentally only one Christian and he *died* on the cross. The 'gospel' died on the Cross. The history of Christianity — after the death on the cross — is the history of a step-by-step and continually grosser misunderstanding of the *original* symbolism. The *church* is that very thing which Jesus preached against — and against which he taught his disciples to fight."

Who is this Jesus for Nietzsche? He wants to reach an approximate classification of Jesus according to psychological type. This can be reached from the Gospels, by rejecting all that which the early Christian community, and especially Paul, invented to add to the story. And then Nietzsche finds a man who did not bring a system or a faith, but who is characterized by his way of life, by acting differently. This action leads Nietzsche to call Jesus the most interesting decadent. Jesus was dominated by his instinctive hate for reality, and by his instinctive rejection of all antipathy and enmity. Nietzsche thus explains why Jesus offered no resistance, suffered patiently, kept silent, was angry at no one, and disdained no one. Jesus was not concerned about the salvation of men, says Nietzsche; he stressed rather how men should live according to these instincts. This becomes possible through a process of rejection of outward reality. Jesus knew only inner realities; and therefore his death had no meaning for him. The kingdom of heaven was not an actual thing, but an attitude of the heart. So, says Nietzsche, began the religion of love.

When the first Christian community was confronted, after the death of Jesus, with the problem of explaining who he was and why he had to die so shameful a death, it produced all sorts of fictions which were added to the true story of Jesus. The Christian community felt that the prevailing Judaism was the real enemy, and that Jesus had been concerned with a revolt against the existing order of things. The community did not want to forgive this death. An innocent person had suffered, God's Son. And God allowed this, the Christian community went on in its fictionalizing, since his Son thus became a sacrifice for the forgiveness of sins. So began the ideas of guilt and punishment, which according to Nietzsche are completely foreign to the psychology of Jesus. That is, what actually was instinct with Jesus, and with his followers, was transmuted into a faith by them. Lies and fictions, says Nietzsche; a decent man will put on gloves before he handles the New Testament, that collection of lies.

It was Paul who took this development and worked it out logically in a system. Paul bears the brunt of Nietzsche's attack. As early as *The Dawn of Day*, Nietzsche devotes a fairly lengthy discussion to Paul. He calls Paul the first Christian. That is noteworthy; Jesus is in the background for Nietzsche; the main attack is directed against Paul. Nietzsche wants to ridicule and destroy Christianity by exposing Paul for what he really was. But later, in *The Antichrist*, Nietzsche discovers Jesus in the background to Paul, and then he knows that he faces a new enemy, the greatest enemy, and an enemy who was a riddle. We have already seen how he tried to solve the riddle.

Let us pause for a moment and examine Nietzsche's interpretation of Paul. Nietzsche pictures him as an epileptic, a master of logic, and a hate-filled man.

The obsession which held Paul in its grip, says Nietzsche, was the fulfillment of the demands of the law. He could not fulfill the law; indeed, he was led through the law to transgression of it.

But once, during an epileptic fit, a light appeared to him. He should no longer persecute Christ in order to fulfill the law; Christ offered a way out; he destroys the power of the law. He is the Savior; he removes all guilt. This is Paul's revenge on life. Christ is risen, and Christians will some day be with Him and be like Him; the hereafter is everything and life is nothing; that is what Paul needed for his boundless lust for power. And then Paul began to adapt the true story of Jesus to these ideas. Even the Old Testament (which Nietzsche elsewhere praises for its incomparable style) was falsified, so that the prophets predict the coming of a Savior. Paul is the perfect example of the priest for Nietzsche. Without him there would have been no Christianity.

How did it come about, then, that Nietzsche had such a perverted idea of Jesus, of Paul, and of Christianity? It must be remembered, in the first place, that the Christianity with which Nietzsche came in contact had little to do with religion, at least in most of its followers. It had become, as Nietzsche himself says, nothing more than a meek moralism, in which aquiescence and modesty had been given divine status. God, freedom, immortality, had given way to amiability and a reasonable disposition; and men believed that these governed the whole cosmos. Only an adulterated form of religion remained, which was honored simply as tradition.

It is understandable that this sham irritated Nietzsche and that he thus rejected Christianity. But he went on to project this sham and pretense on to the whole history of Christianity, so that he would be able to explain the decadence of his time by the decadence of Christianity. That is to say, religion was also a sham for earlier Christians, just as it is in these days; but this sham was finally unmasked and exposed, and the result is the present decadence of culture.

He goes on to make comparisons and establish relationships between the present falsification of reality and what he views as that original falsification in Christianity. "That men now experience sympathetic, disinterested, civilized actions, serving the general welfare as *morality* — that is perhaps the most general result which Christianity has produced in Europe; though this result was not its intention, nor its teaching. But it was the residue of Christian sentiment which remained, a secondary faith in 'love' and 'love your neighbor' which came to the foreground, after the Christian faith, a different thing, egotistical and fundamental faith in 'one thing only is necessary,' in the absolute importance of the eternal *personal* welfare of the individual, in the Christian dogmas — after that faith had receded into the background."

It is clear that Nietzsche's dislike of the decadence and sham he saw around him explains many things; but it does not explain why he judged early Christianity to be a sham as well. The origin of this view lay in himself, in his own *decadence,* and above all in his *atheism.* He cannot believe in God; and that explains his interpretation of Christianity, of Paul, and of Jesus. According to Nietzsche, everything found in Christianity and in Paul which deals with God, heaven, immortality, judgment, is based on lies and is due to the power-lust of the herd and the priests. These lies stood in the way of Nietzsche's ideal of culture, and hence Christianity was his great enemy; and therefore he rejoiced that he thought he could discern the exposure of these lies in his times.

But Jesus would not fit into this framework of ideas. His death on the cross had nothing to do with sham or pretense. Nietzsche was never able to clarify this difficulty, but as he tried to understand Jesus from his atheistic point of view, Jesus could only appear to him as the negation of life and action. In his recontruction of Jesus, many things could not be fitted in: that Jesus could be angered, that he could wield the whip if necessary, that he said he came to bring not peace but a sword, that he castigated the Pharisees, that he knew how to command, that he exercised such a great influence over his disciples that they left everything to follow him. What Nietzsche kept was a weak, suffering, wretched man, a slave type, afraid of life and attracted to death.

This Jesus was Nietzsche's antipode, his last opponent. Nietzsche saw the contrast as one between Jesus' denial of life and his own complete, super-ethical acceptance of life. One can see, then, that Nietzsche's misunderstanding of Jesus originates in his own outlook. As has been correctly noted, the more Nietzsche felt himself to be the Antichrist, the more he viewed Jesus as an anti-Nietzsche, that is as a man who denied life.

Nietzsche could not believe in God, and he logically refused to recognize sin; indeed, he tried to build a culture based on sin. And hence he did not understand, or did not wish to understand, that Jesus was not only a man but also the Son of God; that the decisive thing was not his death, but his resurrection; that the message of the gospel was not his suffering, but the grace that he obtained for all creation on the Cross.

Hence, for Nietzsche, only the failures of Christians in their following of Christ had any reality. This failure was, he said, the gulf between Christ and Christianity. He did not see that in spite of these failures there exists a close tie, the bond of grace, between Christ and his followers; and thus he could not distinguish the fruits of belief.

It would be unjust to Nietzsche to say that he was fully satisfied with his explanation of Jesus. Two things remained in the background of this theory, and they bothered him. One was the deep impression which Jesus had made on Nietzsche, and which could not be reconciled with his theories; and another was the labyrinth into which his own thinking about the acceptance of life and the strong man had brought him.

He could not find God, and did not wish to seek him, because he wanted to keep his faith in man, in himself; he wanted to be a radical humanist. And so he blocked the only way to God, the way that runs by the Cross of Golgotha. For him no way led to God, and that way did not either; but there was still something which was worth some trouble: the Cross; and someone who captivated him: Jesus. Not to such an extent that he would turn to that way in order to search for a solution to his problems. On the contrary, he persevered in searching along the opposite road; but it was there that Jesus appeared to him as his enemy and as his example. He must have understood that he did nothing else but set himself against Jesus and imitate Him.

In any event, it speaks well for his honesty and insight that he not only jeered at Jesus and reviled him, but also continually witnessed to his respect for him. He called him the worst of men; but elsewhere he judges him the noblest. He scoffs at the Cross, that most evil of trees, the most corrupting power; despite this he calls it the most elevating of symbols. To speak of such ideas as hero or genius in connection with Jesus is laughable — a better word is idiot; but he refuses to deny him a place among the "free spirits." Sublime, sick, and child-like: that is the evaluation Nietzsche gives to Jesus; nevertheless Jesus is a forerunner of Zarathustra. Even in Nietzsche's ideal man, which must be the complete opposite of Jesus, this ambivalent attitude persists. "The Superman is a Caesar with the soul of Christ," says Nietzsche in a postscript to *Zarathustra*. "Why did He not remain in the desert, far from the good and rigteous? Perhaps he would have learned to live, and to love the world, and to love life. Believe me, my brothers, he died too soon. If he had reached my age, he would have rejected his own teachings."

When Nietzsche comes to the root of the question, he knows that he must choose between Jesus and himself. And then he becomes the prophet of the Antichrist; then he wants to become the Antichrist himself. He applies *Ecce Homo*, Behold the Man, to himself. It would thus appear as if Nietzsche concerned himself only with Jesus. While he parodied him and sought his opposite, still Nietzsche was in fact nothing else than a parasite feeding on the gospel. Brom has rightly remarked that Zarathustra would be unthinkable without the Bible. The framework, the use of language, the comparisons, the didactic questions, the walks, the search for solitude, the frequent use of texts (literally, paraphrased, or transposed) — all these things which help make of Zarathustra the opponent of the gospel are borrowed from that same gospel.

Nietzsche demolished everything, so that he would not have to capitulate. And when he set about building, he could build *nothing new;* nothing else than a heterogenous mixture of that which Jesus had been and the negation thereof. Did he understand this? At least he spared neither himself nor his readers the disharmony and unintelligibility of his ideal man, the superman; nor did he spare them his passionate restlessness and his convulsiveness. His joy is not real, his soul is never at peace, he never escapes from his problem. Did he realize that the very spirit of gloom he accused Christianity of having actually hung like a leaden cloud over himself? Did he discover that the very resentment from which Christians lived, and on which Christianity was based, according to his notions — that it was this resentment which in the last analysis dominated all of his own work? Gide says, and with good grounds, that Nietzsche can never be understood without considering his jealousy of the gospel.

It is understandable enough that he could develop nothing new, for he sought a way out in the very place to which he knew the self-sovereignty of man would lead him: nihilism. But there is no way in nihilism, and sin has no possibilities on its own.

Even the longing for nihilism can exist only by the grace of that which is not nothing; something that a living God permits to exist by His grace. And therefore Nietzsche faced insoluble riddles, though he believed God was dead. Sin can exist only as a shadow of that which is not sin. And hence Nietzsche, on the road he chose in order to avoid Jesus, encountered Jesus again and again.

Nietzsche wandered to the edge of the abyss, but he walked there with his eyes wide open. Much worse is the decadence of those who wander there with their eyes closed, or those who think they can avoid the problem by taking a safe way far from the chasm. For them, God does not exist even as a problem, and Jesus is not even worth attacking.